YOUR KNOWLEDGE HAS VALUE

- We will publish your bachelor's and
  master's thesis, essays and papers

- Your own eBook and book -
  sold worldwide in all relevant shops

- Earn money with each sale

Upload your text at www.GRIN.com
and publish for free

Ellen Thießen, Maria Schnyder

Conceptual Metaphors of Romantic Love in Western Comic and Japanese Manga

GRIN Verlag

Bibliografische Information der Deutschen Nationalbibliothek:

Die Deutsche Bibliothek verzeichnet diese Publikation in der Deutschen National-bibliografie; detaillierte bibliografische Daten sind im Internet über http://dnb.d-nb.de/ abrufbar.

Dieses Werk sowie alle darin enthaltenen einzelnen Beiträge und Abbildungen sind urheberrechtlich geschützt. Jede Verwertung, die nicht ausdrücklich vom Urheberrechtsschutz zugelassen ist, bedarf der vorherigen Zustimmung des Verla-ges. Das gilt insbesondere für Vervielfältigungen, Bearbeitungen, Übersetzungen, Mikroverfilmungen, Auswertungen durch Datenbanken und für die Einspeicherung und Verarbeitung in elektronische Systeme. Alle Rechte, auch die des auszugsweisen Nachdrucks, der fotomechanischen Wiedergabe (einschließlich Mikrokopie) sowie der Auswertung durch Datenbanken oder ähnliche Einrichtungen, vorbehalten.

Imprint:

Copyright © 2009 GRIN Verlag GmbH
Druck und Bindung: Books on Demand GmbH, Norderstedt Germany
ISBN: 978-3-656-05172-5

This book at GRIN:

http://www.grin.com/en/e-book/181717/conceptual-metaphors-of-romantic-love-in-western-comic-and-japanese-manga

GRIN - Your knowledge has value

Der GRIN Verlag publiziert seit 1998 wissenschaftliche Arbeiten von Studenten, Hochschullehrern und anderen Akademikern als eBook und gedrucktes Buch. Die Verlagswebsite www.grin.com ist die ideale Plattform zur Veröffentlichung von Hausarbeiten, Abschlussarbeiten, wissenschaftlichen Aufsätzen, Dissertationen und Fachbüchern.

Visit us on the internet:

http://www.grin.com/

http://www.facebook.com/grincom

http://www.twitter.com/grin_com

Rijksuniversiteit Groningen

Faculty of Arts

Academic year 2009-2010

Conceptual Metaphors of Romantic Love
in Western Comic and Japanese Manga

by

Ellen Thießen & Maria Schnyder

Paper to the Seminar:

"Language, Communication and Culture"

Winter semester 2009-2010

Closing date: December 17th, 2009

ABSTRACT

1. INTRODUCTION

According to Lakoff and Johnson (1980), metaphors involve a mapping of a tangible source domain on an intangible target domain and enable therefore the expression of concepts difficult to verbalise as such. ROMANTIC LOVE is one of these concepts. Indeed, "romantic love is commonly thought of as a mysterious emotion which it is notoriously difficult to pin down. [...] Various authors in various disciplines have expressed the view that this is a concept that is difficult to grapple with and define" (Kövecses, 1986). By analysing the conceptual metaphors used to describe ROMANTIC LOVE in conventionalised language, Kövesces succeeded to describe the constituents and structure of this concept.

According to Kövecses (2004) the conceptualisation of ROMANTIC LOVE (and EMOTION in general) on a generic level is to a considerable extent universally shared. The universal motivation that enables the metaphors to emerge in different cultures is the shared bodily experience. If metaphors tend to be universal or near-universal on a generic-level, they tend to be different cross-linguistically on a specific level. Kövecses (2004:62) illustrates this theory with the following example: "The HAPPY IS UP metaphor is a generic-level metaphor. [...] a specific-level version of the metaphor HAPPY IS UP in English is HAPPINESS IS BEING OFF THE GROUND. [...] this specific metaphor does not exist in Chinese". The causes of cross cultural metaphor variation on a specific level are mainly differential experience, cultural context, history and experiential focus (Kövecses, 2004:68-74).

Yeşim Aksan and Dilek Kantar's (2008) research on the cross-cultural perspective of love metaphors in English and Turkish align with the theory of Kövecses (2004). The English and Turkish culture shares indeed the FORCE and PATH image schemas. However, the entailments of the metaphors reveal major differences in the conception of romantic love. The differential experience and cultural memory are reflected in the opposition of the active, goal- and success-oriented, and collaborative perspective of the English culture and the passive, non-goal- and not success-oriented, and solitary perspective of the Turkish culture. Furthermore, LOVE IS PAIN/SUFFERING is the prototypical love model in Turkish, probably motivated by the culture-specific myth of "Laila and Majnum" and the Sufi philosophy. Suffering for love is on the contrary a nonprototypical love model in English, mainly expressed by the conceptual metaphor of LOVE IS A DISEASE.

Kövecses research on the concept of ROMANTIC LOVE and the cultural variation of metaphor is based exclusively on verbal evidence. As Charles Forceville (2005:69) acknowledged, "in the interest of enriching insights into ideological conceptual metaphors, non-verbal and multimedial representations need to be investigated as well"; mostly in order to break "the vicious cycle of saying that verbal metaphoric expressions are evidence of conceptual metaphors, and then saying that we know that because we see conceptual metaphors expressed in language" (Cienki, 1998). The present paper aims to extend Kövecses research by analysing the visual expression of

ROMANTIC LOVE and its cross-cultural variation in comics. Indeed, as Forceville (2005:71) mentioned, "comics are a good source of pictorial data for such a project: unlike, for instance, realistic photographs and live-action films, which are more or less 'naturally' mirror real-life manifestations of emotions, comics and cartoons make use of stereotypical exaggerations and of a rudimentary 'sign-system' very much like a language". To analyse pictorial metaphors, two categories of visual signs are considered: indexial signs and pictorial runes. Indexial signs are defined as symptoms that we often perceive in daily life as accompanying a certain emotion. These are metonymic rather than metaphorical: for example, *blushing* stands for ROMANTIC LOVE of the person metonymically. Pictorial runes are not based on observations of daily life but are part of the pictorial language to express a certain emotion: as example, Forceville analyses the representation of smoke as a pictorial rune for anger, based on the metaphor THE ANGRY PERSON IS A PRESSURIZED CONTAINER.

In a first part, our paper will show how Kövecses' characterisation of the concept of ROMANTIC LOVE surfaces visually in the comic *Asterix*. The second part of this paper aims to explore this cross-cultural variation in the visual domain by comparing the results of the analysis of *Asterix* to Japanese Manga. Our research will be done on following data: three volumes of German translations of the French comic *Asterix Asterix* (*Asterix als Legionär (Vol. 10), Asterix und Latraviata (Vol. 31)*, and *Obelix auf Kreuzfahrt (Vol. 30)*) and the Japanese manga *I"s* (Vol. 7), *Tsubasa* (Vol. 13), *Natsuki Takaya* (Vol. 3). In all of these comics, romantic love plays an essential role. The traditional comic of Asterix and Obelix tells the story of two Galliards, who are always in war with other nations. In the chosen comics Obelix' object of love is Falbala, a beautiful girl of the village, who is engaged with Tragicomix. These three comics are the only ones where she plays an essential role. *I"s* tells the story of Ichitas who is secretly in love with Iori, whose feelings aren't revealed at that point of the story. In *Natsuki Takaya*, Yun Yun, Yuki and Kyo are popular teenage boys and the objects of love of a group of immature, childish girls. Shaolan and Sakura are the protagonists of *Tsubasa*: to live their love, they first have to travel across different dimension to collect the "feathers of memory".

2. KÖVECSES' CONCEPT OF ROMANTIC LOVE

Kövecses (1986: 61-105) identified LOVE IS A UNITY (OF TWO COMPLEMENTARY PARTS) as central metaphor of the concept of ROMANTIC LOVE. This metaphor is motivated by the supposed similarity between certain love experiences and the unity of two complementary physical, chemical, etc. parts. This implies that ideal love is mutual and equal in degree; concept that is represented as well by the LOVE IS A VALUABLE COMMODITY (IN AN ECONOMIC EXCHANGE) metaphor. The conception of love as UNITY OF TWO COMPLEMENTARY PARTS considers love as some kind of need. This idea is reflected in the metaphor THE OBJECT OF LOVE IS (APPETIZING) FOOD. Nevertheless, we eat appetizing food not only to satisfy a need, but we enjoy it, we like it. LIKING is therefore a related concept to ROMANTIC LOVE. LIKING is not the only emotional concept closely linked to the one of ROMANTIC LOVE. Kövecses describes that ROMANTIC LOVE presupposes, or takes as granted the presence of the concepts of AFFECTION, ENTHUSIASME, INTEREST, INTIMACY, and LIKING. Related on to the concept of ROMANTIC LOVE, but not considered to be inherent to it are DEVOTION and SACRIFICE, and in a looser way FRIENDSHIP, SEXUAL DESIRE, RESPECT, and KINDNESS. Kövecses also identifies a casual relationship between the concepts of LOVE and HAPPINESS.

THE BODY IS A CONTAINER FOR THE EMOTIONS metaphor allows the conceptualization of INTENSITY as AMOUNT, or QUANTITY (INSIDE A CONTAINER). In love, this means that the more fluid there is in the container, the more intense is love. A variation of the CONTAINER metaphor is LOVE IS IN THE HEART, where the heart is a container with blood as a fluid pumping through it; the heart can therefore be considered to be the seat of the emotion of love. The major way of conceptualizing love's intensity is HEAT. HEAT manifests itself primarily in the LOVE IS FIRE metaphor. The entailments of this metaphor teach us the following thing of the concept of LOVE: since the thing burned is unable to function normally, a person in love is unable to function normally. Another entailment leads us to the concept of EMOTIONAL PAIN, considering that fire can burn us and cause pain. The physical experiences of getting burned by fire structures the emotional pain caused by love.

According to Kövecses (1986:87), following physiological effects are assumed by our folk model to accompany love: *increased body heat, increased heart rate, blushing*, and *interference with accurate perception*. Furthermore, the model shows that *as love increases, its physiological effects increase* and that *there is a limit beyond which the physiological effects impair normal functioning*, where the metonymic principle implies that *the physiological effects of an emotion stand for the emotion*.

The lover is considered to be a passive object that undergoes love. The emotion appears to be A NATURAL FORCE, A PHYSICAL FORCE (MAGNETIC, CHEMICAL, GRAVITATIONAL, etc.) or MAGIC. The lack of control of the lover is besides the earlier named metaphor LOVE IS INTERFERENCE WITH ACCURATE PERCEPTION represented by LOVE IS INSANITY and LOVE IS A RAPTURE.

The passivity of the lover in the ideal love model conflicts with different concepts of the typical love model. First of all, it is contradicted by the concept of LOVE IS A HIDDEN OBJECT. Within this concept, love is not coming along; instead we must go out and find it. The concepts of LOVE IS A GAME and LOVE IS WAR confirm the more active role of the lover. Furthermore, the lover doesn't tolerate his lack of control over love, but fights it: LOVE IS AN OPPONENT. Considering that LOVE IS A CAPTIVE ANIMAL and a BEAST INSIDE A PERSON, and can therefore cause harm to others and to ourselves, to control the emotion of love is primordial.

3. Metaphors of Romantic Love in Asterix

In this chapter the different metaphors in *Asterix* will be pointed out, analyzed, also with regard to their creative illustrations, and compared with Kövecses' data basis of conceptual metaphors of romantic love. First of all the LOVE IS UNITY metaphor will be observed, afterwards THE BODY IS A CONTAINER FOR THE EMOTIONS metaphor, the LOVE IS A HOT FLUID IN A CONTAINER metaphor and as well how *the physiological effects of love impair normal functioning*. Besides the LOVE IS A COMPETITION metaphor will be taken into account and finally the metaphors of LOVE IS KINDNESS and LOVE IS HAPPINESS.

3.1 LOVE IS UNITY

The central metaphor of the concept of romantic love, LOVE IS UNITY, implies that the lovers are two equal parts, which need each other and can't live without each other. In *"Asterix als Legionär"* this metaphor can be found in two different pictures. Figure 1 and 2 is showing Falbala, who is shocked and crying because her fiancé Tragicomix is abducted, and figure 2 shows Obelix crying, because he noticed that Falbala has a fiancé. The grounded metaphor is THE PHYSICAL ABSENCE OF LOVE IS PAIN. The other part is needed to be a "whole". The indexial signs are open mouth (1/1), wide-open eyes (1/2) and the hand in the face (1/3) for shock and anxiety; crying with the face lying in the hands (figure 2/1) and a sagged Obelix crying in the arms of Asterix (figure 3/1). The bold face and the jagged line in the text balloon as pictorial signals underline this. The bold face letters (figure 3/2) expresses the loudness of the spoken unhappiness. The jagged line (figure 1/4) also aims at the primary effect of expressing loudness and emphasis of Falbala's disappointment, fear and pain.

Fig. 1: Falbala. Signs of pain:
(1) open mouth, (2) wide-open eyes,
(3) hand in the face, (4) jagged line
(from *Asterix als Legionär*)

Fig. 2: Falbala, Asterix, Obelix.
Signs of pain: (1) crying with the face in the
hands (from *Asterix als Legionär*)

Fig. 3: Obelix, Asterix, villager.

Signs of pain: (1) sagged Obelix crying in the arms of Asterix, (2) bold face letters (from *Asterix als Legionär*)

3.2 THE BODY IS THE CONTAINER FOR EMOTIONS

Furthermore Kövesces identified THE BODY IS A CONTAINER FOR THE EMOTIONS metaphor. A variation of the CONTAINER metaphor is the more basic LOVE IS IN THE HEART, where heart is the seat of the emotion of love. In *Asterix* we can also find the complementary metaphor UNHAPPY LOVE IS BROKEN HEART. In figure 4/1 and 5/1 Obelix is surrounded by hearts expressing his love as pictorial rune. The hearts are the container of his emotions. This container can be broken when the love is one-sided and thus unhappy (figure 6/1). The unhappy love is furthermore supported by Obelix's facial expressions. His wide open eyes underline his shock and pain (figure 6/2).

Fig. 4: Falbala, Asterix, Obelix. Signs of love: (1) hearts around Obelix (from *Asterix als Legionär*)

Fig. 5: Asterix, Falbala, Obelix. Signs of love: (1) big heart (from *Asterix als Legionär*)

Fig. 6: Asterix, Falbala, Obelix. Signs of unhappy love: (1) broken heart, (2) wide open eyes (from *Asterix als Legionär*)

3.3 LOVE IS A HOT FLUID IN A CONTAINER

As already mentioned, the major way of conceptualizing love's intensity is HEAT. HEAT manifests itself primarily in the LOVE IS FIRE metaphor. We can also find this conceptual metaphor in *Asterix*. According to Kövecses (1986:87), physiological effects like *increased body heat* or *blushing* are connected to this LOVE IS FIRE metaphor. In figure 7/1, 8/1 and 9/1 we can see Asterix and Obelix with blushed faces. The wide open eyes (7/2 and 8/2) underline their overheated, congealed body state. In figure 9/2 there are also pictorial runes of smoke above Obelix's head. It can't be interpreted as a realistic source in the story and thus has to be the smoke of the already boiling hot fluid in the container, based on THE LOVING PERSON IS A PRESSURIZED CONTAINER metaphor.

Fig. 7: Tragicomix, Falbala, Asterix. Signs of Love: (1) blushing, (2) wide open eyes (from *Asterix als Legionär*)

Fig. 8: Tragicomix, Falbala, Obelix. Signs of love: (1) blushing, (2) wide open eyes (from *Asterix als Legionär*)

Fig. 9: Falbala, Obelix. Signs of love: (1) blushing, (2) smoke (from *Asterix und Latraviata*)

3.4 THE PHYSIOLOGICAL EFFECTS OF LOVE IMPAIR NORMAL FUNCTIONING

3.4.1   LOVE IS UNCONTROLLED POWER

Furthermore *as love increases, its physiological effects increase* and *these physiological effects impair normal functioning*. This conceptual metaphor is illustrated in *Asterix* in a very creative way. LOVE IS UNCONTROLLED POWER: The strong Obelix loses control of his body and immense power. He is running against trees and so roots them out (figure 10/1) or he is kicking at a tree and so cuts the tree down (figure 11/1). The onomatopoeic use of "Kracks" (fig. 10/2 and 11/2) to visualize the uprooting of trees underlines the intensity of the uncontrolled power.

Fig. 10: Obelix, Asterix, Falbala, Miraculix. Signs of love: (1) running against trees, (2) onomatopoeia "Kracks" (from *Asterix als Legionär*)

Fig. 11: Asterix, Obelix. Signs of love: (1) disrooting trees, (2) onomatopoeia "Kracks" (from *Asterix als Legionär*)

3.4.2 LOVE IS UNCONTROLLED BODY LANGUAGE

The lover can lose control of his or her body as another physiological effect of love. It could be said, that *the impossibility of controlling emotion is the impossibility of controlling the body*. The physiological effects can be defined as *nervous playing with the hands or the feet*. When Asterix talks about Falbala Obelix is shaking his head heavily (figure 12/1, left) while his hands are emphatically close to his body (figure 12/2, both) or even hidden behind his back (figure 13/1). Whilst his hands are close to his body, he is playing with his fingers and so showing his nervousness, shyness and queasy feeling (figure 12/3). In figure 13/2 he is also playing with his feet on the ground.

Fig. 12: Asterix, Obelix. Signs of love: (1) head shaking, (2) hands close to his body, (3) playing with fingers (from *Asterix als Legionär*)

Fig. 13: Obelix, Asterix. Signs of love: (1) hidden hands, (2) playing with feet (from *Asterix als Legionär*)

3.4.3 LOVE IS INABILITY TO FUNCTION NORMALLY

The impossibility to function normally is illustrated by *the inability to eat, to move* and *to speak*. In figure 14 we can see Obelix, who can't eat more than two wild pigs (1). He is dreaming and looking up (2). The text balloon of Obelix looks like a cloud underlining the dreaming as a pictorial rune (14/3) and also the capital-letters in "GROSSER SEUFZER" (engl. *deep-drawn sigh*) express the intensity of his feelings (14/4).

Fig. 14: Asterix, Obelix. Signs of love: (1) stopped eating, (2) dreaming and looking up, (3) cloud text balloon, (4) capital-letters in text balloon (from *Asterix als Legionär*)

The *inability to move* and *to speak* is shown by the following figure, where Obelix is staying with a congealed body (1) and wide opened, starring eyes (2) facing his object of love. He can't move, but also can't talk. In the text balloon the consonants "Wkrstksft" make no sense and show that Obelix lost his ability to talk (3).

Fig. 15: Miraculix, Asterix, Falbala, Obelix. Signs of love:
(1) congealed body, (2) wide opened eyes, (3) strange language in text balloon (from *Asterix als Legionär*)

Also Kövecses' (1986) metaphor LOVE IS INTERFERENCE WITH ACCURATE PERCEPTION can be found in *Asterix*. In figure 16 we can see Obelix forgetting his task (bringing the wild pigs to Asterix) when he sees Falbala. He is so focused on her that his perception is totally limited (16/1). The effect of love is therefore also affecting the memory. His wide open eyes underline his focusing (16/2).

Fig. 16: Asterix, Obelix, Falbala. Signs of love: (1) focusing of beloved object, (2) wide open eyes (from *Asterix als Legionär*)

3.4.4   LOVE IS MAGIC

The last subdivision of the physiological effects of love can be explained by the lover, who is considered to be a passive object that undergoes love, which appears to be *magic*. In *Obelix auf Kreuzfahrt* Obelix is bewitched into a stone. Miraculix thinks that he can be transmogrified when his object of love is kissing him (figure 17). The grounded metaphor is LOVE IS MAGIC or even *love is assumed to be stronger than magic*. But in this example it doesn't work out. After the kiss Obelix is still a stone and Falbala leaves humbled. Thus the power of love is still limited, but the metaphorical comparison of love and magic exists in this comic.

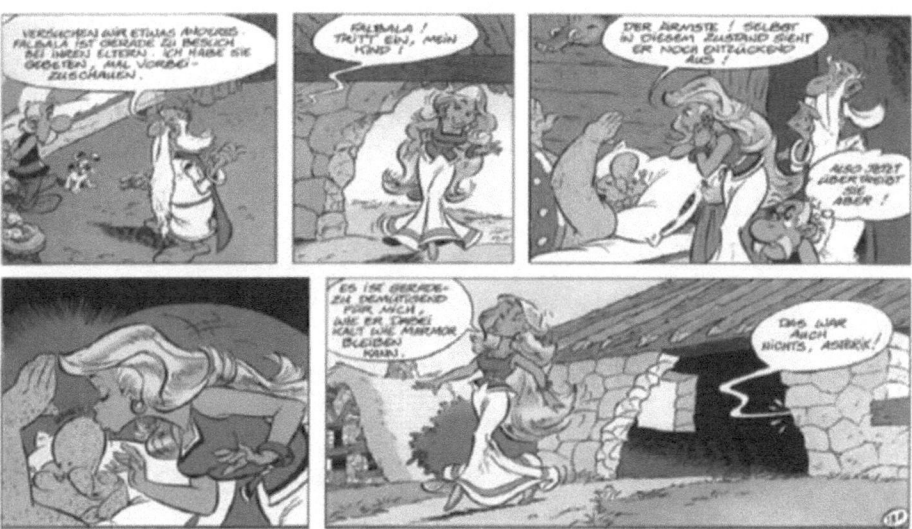

Fig. 17: Miraculix, Asterix, Falbala, Obelix (from *Obelix auf Kreuzfahrt*)

Another example of love as magic can be seen in figure 18, 19 and 20. In the 18th figure we see Obelix looking at Falbala (1) and "shining" of positive emotion (2). He seems to be hypnotized by his loving object and passive in the real world. The stars around his head are pictorial runes underlining his bewitched or hypnotized state and his mental absence. The illustration shows that the *lover is hypnotized by his object of love*.

Fig. 18: Miraculix, Falbala, Asterix, Obelix. Signs of love: (1) focussing the beloved object, (2) stars around Obelix's head (from *Asterix als Legionär*)

Another illustration of the hypnotizing effect of the object of love can be seen in figure 19 and 20. Asterix and Obelix have a *hypnotized facial expression* (19/1 and 20/1) and *follow their object of love blindly* and without any noticeable own action.

Fig. 19: Obelix, Falbala. Signs of love: (1) abscene look, (2) blind following (from *Asterix und Latraviata*)

Fig. 20: Falbala, Asterix.
Signs of love: (1) hypnotized
eyes, (2) blind following
(from *Asterix und Latraviata*)

3.5 LOVE IS A COMPETITION

The more active role of the lover can be found in the concepts of LOVE IS A COMPETITION. This concept is illustrated in the two following figures. In figure 21 Obelix is shown next to Tragicomix, the fiancée of Falbala and so his biggest concurrent. He doesn't face his concurrent, but makes a critical face (21/1), expressing incredulity and hostility. To underline this, Obelix has his hands hidden behind his back (21/2), disrupt physical contact with the enemy and ready to fight for his love. Another kind of competition can be found in figure 22/1. The girls of the village apply for the love of Asterix and are therefore staying in a row, presenting themselves.

Fig. 21: Asterix, Tragicomix, Obelix. Signs of love: (1) critical facial expression of Obelix, (2) hidden hands (from *Asterix der Legionär*)

Fig. 22: Asterix, Asterix's mother, girls from the village. Signs of love: (1) girls standing in a row (from *Asterix und Latraviata*)

In figure 23 the two friends are fighting for the same object of love (1). Both have a red face (2) and are shouting at each other with clenched fists (4). The pictorial rune of the bold face and jagged line in the text balloons (3) as well as the onomatopoetic use of "Paff" (5), describing the sound of the beat, express the intensity of this fight.

Fig. 23: Obelix, Asterix, Falbala. Signs of love: (1) shouting and fighting, (2) red face, (3) bold face and jagged line in text balloon, (4) clenched fists, (5) onomatopoeic "Paff" (from *Asterix und Latraviata*)

3.6 LOVE IS HAPPINESS

The conceptual metaphor LOVE IS HAPPINESS defined by Kövesces together with HAPPINESS IS BEING OFF THE GROUND can be combined as: *love is being off the ground*. In figure 24 Tragicomix is shown when he hears that he will see Falbala again and thus is happy, which is expressed through jumping and smiling.

Fig. 24: Asterix, Tragicomix, Obelix. Signs of love: (1) jumping, (2) smiling (from *Asterix als Legionär*)

3.7 LOVE IS KINDNESS

Finally Kövecses identified the metaphor LOVE IS KINDNESS. An illustration of this metaphor can be found in figure 25, where we can see Obelix with a big stone with a bow in his hand, which is a present for Falbala.

Fig. 25: Asterix, Obelix. Signs of love: (1) Obelix with a stone as present (from *Asterix als Legionär*)

4. Previous studies Japanese manga

Kazuko Shinohara and Yoshihiro Matsunaka (2009) analyzed pictorial metaphors of emotion, and especially anger, in Japanese manga. They confirmed Forceville's thesis (2005): the two basic metaphors ANGER IS A HOT FLUID IN A CONTAINER and EMOTION IS FORCE are also present in visual modalities. The last one of these two metaphors is nevertheless elaborated in a different way at a more specific level in the Japanese culture. Indeed, the analysis of manga confirmed that in Japanese, EMOTION IS EXTERNAL METEOROLOGICAL/NATURAL PHENOMENON THAT SURROUNDS THE SELF. Shinohara and Matsunaka supported the existence of the meteorological metaphor with examples of illustrations of the feelings of anger, disappointment and surprise. Love and happiness is considered to be represented by the natural phenomenon of flowers and birds.

5. Metaphors of ROMANTIC LOVE in Japanese Manga

5.1 THE BODY IS A CONTAINER FOR THE EMOTION

THE BODY IS A CONTAINER FOR THE EMOTIONS metaphor is not only in the *Asterix* comics, but also in the analyzed mangas the most frequent basic metaphor for ROMANTIC LOVE. The universality of this metaphor earlier demonstrated by Kövecses (2004) is therefore confirmed by our pictorial database. This metaphor is visualized by its physiological effects; since *the physiological effects of an emotion stand for the emotion*. Similar to Asterix, *blushing* is a generalized visual expression of the feeling of ROMANTIC LOVE (figure 26).

Fig. 26: Yuki and Toru. Signs of blushing (from *Fruit Basket*).

Additionally to *blushing*, the *increased body heat* is represented in the manga by signs of facial *sweat* (figures 27-31). Another physiological effect that is not present in the Asterix comic is the *increased heart rate* (figures 27-34), expressed in the manga by the onomatopoeias "poch", "boch" and "bobom". In all of the examples, Kövecses' hypothesis (1986) of *as love increases, its physiological effects increase* is confirmed.

Fig. 27-31: Ichitas. Signs of sweat and increased heart rate (from *I''s*).

Fig. 32-34: Ichitas and Iori. Signs of increased heart rate (from *I''s*).

The facial expression of the person showing signs of *blushing*, *sweat* and *increased heart rate* is in several cases signed by a distorted mouth and wide-open eyes, expression for anxiety and stress. Therefore, these physiological effects seem in the present case only indirectly connected to ROMANTIC LOVE: via the concepts of ANXIETY and STRESS. This implies that these two concepts have a casual relationship with the concept of ROMANTIC LOVE, similar to the concept of HAPPINESS (Kövecses, 1986:80). We suggest adding ANXIETY and STRESS to the typical love model established by Kövecses (1986:103), at least for the Japanese culture. It would be necessary to do research on the connection between the concepts of ANXIETY and STRESS and the concept of ROMANTIC LOVE in the western culture, since none of these signs are found in the *Asterix* data.

The suggestion of considering ANXIETY and STRESS as to ROMANTIC LOVE connected concepts is also motivated by other observations. While in *Asterix* the lover feels the irresistible need to look at its object of love, in several situations in the Japanese manga, he is unable or refuses to look at her (figures 35-38). This could be related to the typical love model of Kövecses (1986:103) according to whom, the lover doesn't tolerate his lack of control over love, but fights it (LOVE IS AN OPPONENT). Indeed, not looking at the object of love increases the lover's chances to control its emotion of love, and most of all the level of STRESS and its physiological effects.

Fig. 35-36: Ichitas and Yori. Ichitas not looking at Iori (from *I''s*).

Fig. 37-38: Ichitas and Yori. Ichitas not looking at Iori (from *I''s*).

The existence of ANXIETY as a related concept to ROMANTIC LOVE would be motivated by the metaphor EMOTION IS EXTERNAL METEOROLOGICAL/NATURAL PHENOMENON THAT SURROUNDS THE SELF. Indeed, the expression of the lovers *increased heart rate* is accompanied by a dark cloudy sky (figures 39-40). According to Kazuko Shinohara and Yoshihiro Matsunaka (2009), darkness is a pictorial rune for ANXIETY.

Fig. 39-40: Ichitas. Dark clouds as signs for anxiety (from *I''s*).

5.2. THE PHYSIOLOGICAL EFFECTS OF LOVE IMPAIR NORMAL FUNCTIONING

Just like in *Asterix*, the *physiological effects of love that impair normal functioning* are expressed by the lover's nervous play with his hands (figures 41-45).

Fig. 41-42: Kimi and Yun Yun. Nervous playing with the fingers (from *Fruit Basket*).

Fig. 43: Yuki, Toru and scholar. Nervous playing with the fingers (from *Fruit Basket*).

Fig. 44: Yuki and scholars. Nervous playing with the fingers (from *Fruit Basket*).

Fig. 45: Ichitas and Yori. Nervous playing with the fingers (from *I"s*).

5.3. LOVE IS HAPPINESS

The concept of HAPPINESS, casually connected to the concept of ROMANTIC LOVE (Kövecses, 1986:80), is like in *Asterix* visually represented in the Japanese mangas. Indeed, in numerous situations the person in love is expressing through a bright smile and sometimes closed eyes his HAPPINESS, most often while being in the direct entourage of the object of love (figures 46-53). The more specific metaphor LOVE IS BEEING OFF THE GROUND present in *Asterix* is absent from the Japanese manga.

Fig. 46: Shaolan. Signs of happiness (from *Tsubasa*).

Fig. 47: Ichitas. Signs of happiness (from *I"s*).

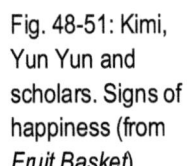

Fig. 48-51: Kimi, Yun Yun and scholars. Signs of happiness (from *Fruit Basket*).

Fig. 52-53: Yuki and Toru. Signs of happiness (from *Fruit Basket*)

5.4. LOVE IS DESIRE

One occurrence is representing visually the concept of SEXUAL DESIRE, that is according to Kövecses (1986:77) connected to our idea of ROMANTIC LOVE. The emotion is represented by the lover staring with extremely enlarged eyes at the girl's underwear (figure 54).

Fig. 54: Ichitas and Yori. Signs of sexual desire (from *I"s*).

- 17 -

5.5. LOVE IS FOWERS

The metaphor LOVE IS FLOWERS (Shinohara, Matsunaka 2009:285), based on the EMOTION IS EXTERNAL METEOROLOGICAL/NATURAL PHENOMENON THAT SURROUNDS THE SELF metaphor and represented by the pictorial rune of little flowers surrounding the person in love, can be observed in one occurrence (figure 55).

Fig. 55: Yuki and Toru. Flowers as sign for love (from *Fruit Basket*).

6. CONCLUSION

The aim of this paper was to analyse the visual concepts of romantic love in Western comics and Japanese Manga. As a basis the concept of ROMANTIC LOVE of Kövecses provided the theoretical terms. To summarize this research, it has to be pointed out, that in *Asterix* (as a traditional and well-known example of Western comics) a lot of conceptual metaphors can be found. Most frequently THE BODY IS A CONTAINER FOR THE EMOTIONS, LOVE IS A HOT FLUID IN A CONTAINER metaphors and the different *physiological effects of love that impair normal functioning* could be found in the three *Asterix* comics. Besides and less regularly we can find the metaphors LOVE IS UNITY, LOVE IS A COMPETITION and LOVE IS KINDNESS / HAPPINESS. All of these metaphors are often illustrated in a creative way. Some examples of these creative illustrations, which were exposed within this paper, are *the lover is disrooting trees, love is nervous playing with the hands and/or the feet, love effects the memory* and *the object of love has a hypnotizing effect on the lover.*

Moreover we looked at the indexial signs as well as the pictorial runes, as the two modes of visual realizations in comics. To sum up indexial signs are used, just as *blushing, nervous playing with the hands*, the *hypnotized lover* etc., which represents the western folk model of love, based on observations in reality. Additionally, we can find lots of pictorial runes, which emphasize the metaphors clearly and play with the "traditional" conceptual metaphors of ROMANTIC LOVE, just like the smoke expresses the already boiling fluid in the container, based on the metaphor THE LOVING PERSON IS A PRESSURIZED CONTAINER.

Furthermore, the cross-cultural variation was taken into consideration by comparing *Asterix* to Japanese manga. The culture-specific metaphor LOVE IS FLOWERS, analyzed by Shinohara and Matsunaka (2009), can be confirmed. Manga shares with *Asterix* the basic metaphors of ROMANTIC LOVE: THE BODY IS A CONTAINER FOR THE

EMOTIONS and LOVE IS A HOT FLUID IN A CONTAINER. *Blushing* is just like in *Asterix* one of the dominant physiological effects of ROMANTIC LOVE. Additionally, manga insists on the physiological effect of *increased heart rate* and *sweat*. As we discussed, in the presented cases these physiological effects don't seem to be inherent in the concept of ROMANTIC LOVE; they are rather signs of STRESS and ANXIETY. This hypothesis is supported by following observations: The lover feels a high level of stress while being in the surroundings of his object of love and tries to control this emotion by not looking directly at the person. The hypothesis that ANXIETY is the second essential reason for *increased heart rate* and signs of *sweat* is supported by the combination of these signs with the representation of darkness, which is according to the culture-specific metaphor EMOTION IS AN EXTERNAL METEOROLOGICAL/NATURAL PHENOMENON THAT SURROUNDS THE SELF the expression of ANXIETY. Therefore, we suggest considering these concepts as casually related to ROMANTIC LOVE, similar to HAPPINESS.

In the comic of *Asterix*, the concept of ANXIETY and STRESS is not related to the concept of ROMANTIC LOVE. Further research would be necessary to verify if this link between the concepts is culture-specific, and if yes which cultural features of Japan motivate it.

6. REFERENCES

1. Aksan, Y., Kantar, D. (2008), "No Wellness Feels Better than This Sickness: Love Metaphors from a Cross-Cultural Perspective", in: *Metaphor and Symbol*, 23, pp.262-291.

2. Cienki, A. (1998), "Metaphoric gestures and some of their relations to verbal metaphoric expressions", in: Koenig, J.-P. (Ed.), *Discourse and Cognition: Bridging the Gap*, Stanford, CSLI, pp. 189-204.

3. Forceville, Ch. (2005), "Visual representations of the idealized cognitive model of *anger* in the Asterix album *La Zizanie*, in: *Journal of Pragmatics*, 37:1, pp.69-88.

4. Kövecses, Z. (2000), "Cultural variation in the conceptualization of emotion", in: *Metaphor and Emotion: Language, Culture, and Body in Human Feeling*, Cambridge, Cambridge University Press, pp.164-181.

5. Kövecses, Z. (2004), "Cultural variation in metaphor" in: *European Journal of English Studies*, 8:3, pp.267-274.

6. Kövecses, Z. (1986), *Metaphors of Anger, Pride and Love*, Amsterdam/Philadelphia, Benjamins.

7. Lakoff, G., Johnson, M. (1980), *Metaphors We Live By*, Chicago, University of Chicago Press.

8. Shinohara, K., Matsunaka, Y. (2009), "Pictorial metaphors of emotion in Japanese comics", in: Forceville, J., *Multimodal Metaphor*, Berlin, Mouton de Gruyter.